TO FORGET THE SELF

An Illustrated Guide to Zen Meditation

The Zen Writings Series

To study the Buddha way
is to study the self.

To study the self
is to forget the self.

To forget the self
is to be enlightened by all things.

To Forget the Self

An Illustrated Guide to Zen Meditation

John Daishin Buksbazen
Photography by John Daido Loori

Foreword by Peter Matthiessen
Preface by Chotan Aitken Roshi

ZEN WRITINGS SERIES.

On Zen Practice: The Foundations of Practice
On Zen Practice II: Body, Breath and Mind
To Forget the Self: An Illustrated Guide to
Zen Meditation
Enlightenment: On Zen Practice III (1978)

Series Editors: Hakuyu Taizan Maezumi, Bernard Tetsugen Glassman
Publishing Editor: John Daishin Buksbazen
Editors for this volume: Stephan Ikkō Bodian, Helen Glassman
Design: John Daidō Loori
Graphics Staff: Jan Norris, Larry Watson, Fran Ziegler

To Forget the Self is one volume in the Zen Writings series, a monographic series comprising two new titles a year with occasional supplementary releases. Subscription rate for two volumes a year: $10.00 in the U.S., $15.00 foreign. For information about subscriptions or distribution, contact: Zen Writings, 927 South Normandie Avenue, Los Angeles, California 90006, ISBN: 0-916820-03-3. Library of Congress Catalog Number: 76-9475. Published by Zen Center of Los Angeles, Inc., 927 South Normandie Avenue, Los Angeles, California 90006, a non-profit religious corporation. Copyright © 1977 by Zen Center of Los Angeles, Inc. All rights reserved. Printed in the United States of America.

Thanks to the publishers for permission to reprint quotations from the following books:

Minor White, *Mirrors, Messages, Manifestations*. Copyright © 1969 by Aperture, Inc. Reprinted by permission of Aperture, Inc.

Zenkei Shibayama, *Zen Comments on the Mumonkan*. Copyright 1974 by Harper & Row. Reprinted by permission of Harper & Row.

Shunryu Suzuki, *Zen Mind, Beginner's Mind*. Copyright © 1970 by John Weatherhill, Inc. Reprinted by permission of Zen Center and John Weatherhill, Inc.

Printed in the United States of America by Thomson-Shore Co., Michigan, on Warren Lustro offset enamel. Text typeface is Palatino set by Chapman's Phototypesetting, Fullerton, Calif.

This book is dedicated to my teachers,
parents, wife, country
and all beings everywhere.

CONTENTS

LIST OF ILLUSTRATIONS

Historically, explanations and expositions of practice were a rarity to beginning Zen students. But early in this century, Daiun Sōgaku Harada Roshi, a Japanese Zen master regarded far and wide as one of the finest, felt that modern times had created an authentic need for new Zen students to have a clearer intellectual understanding of their practice. Accordingly he created a series of eleven lectures (the *sōzan* talks) designed to provide such an introduction to practice.

His successor, Hakuun Yasutani Roshi, and Yasutani Roshi's successor, Taizan Maezumi Roshi, have continued this tradition and have brought it to this continent. For the past eight years, as a student of Maezumi Roshi's, I have been giving a series of talks and seminars based upon these *sōzan* talks, aimed at a heterogeneous American audience. It was out of this experience that *To Forget the Self* was conceived. It does not attempt to cover all the ground of the *sōzan* talks, but has grown out of them, focussing on a few key issues, presenting them as simply and conversationally as possible.

In writing this book, I found that the critical and encouraging comments of the many readers were of great help to me. Their assistance was invaluable, and I count them as collaborators in this work. Especially significant were the contributions of Steve Ikko Bodian, Helen Glassman, Tetsugen Glassman Sensei, Ed Kenzan Levin and Paul Genki Kahn. Additionally, I am deeply indebted to John Daidō Loori, whose visual baby

ACKNOWLEDGEMENTS

this book is. These are a few of the very key people who helped directly in shaping the book; there are many others who must go unnamed, but to all of them I offer my deep thanks.

Finally, my teacher, Taizan Maezumi Roshi, must be gratefully appreciated for his generous vision and patience through the years.

This gentle book, reflecting the wise teachings of Taizan Maezumi Roshi, is a wonderful introduction to Zen Buddhism, and also an invitation to new life. To practice Zen means to realize one's existence in the beauty and clarity of this present moment, rather than letting life unravel in useless daydreaming of the past and future. To "rest in the present" is a state of magical simplicity, although attainment of this state is not as simple as it sounds: most of us need dedicated training under the guidance of a roshi (Zen master) in order to let the debris of existence fall away. From the very beginning, the sitting meditation called zazen will bring about a strong sense of well-being, as body and mind return to natural harmony with all Creation; later there comes true insight into the nature of existence, which is no different from one's own true nature, or the nature of the Buddha—"He-Who-Knows."

Zen has been called "the religion before religion," which is to say that anyone can practice, even those committed to another faith. And the phrase evokes that natural religion of our early childhood, when heaven and a splendorous earth were one. For the new child in the light of spring, there is no self to forget; the eye with which he sees God, in Meister Eckhart's phrase, is the eye with which God sees him. But that clear eye is soon clouded over by ideas and opinions, preconceptions and abstractions, and simple *being* becomes encrusted with the armor of the ego. Not until years later does an instinct come that a vital sense of mystery has been withdrawn. The sun glints through the pines, and the heart is pierced in a moment of beauty and strange pain, like a memory of paradise.

After that day, there is no beauty without pain, and at the bottom of each breath, there is a hollow place that is filled with longing. That day we become seekers without knowing that we seek, and at first, we long for something "greater" than ourselves, something far away. It is not a return to childhood, for childhood is not a truly enlightened state; yet to seek one's own true nature is, as one Zen master has said, "a way to lead you to your long-lost home."

Most of us cast about for years until something in our reading, some stray word, points to the vague outlines of a path. Perhaps this book is the beginning of your homeward way; if so, count yourself lucky, for it offers no tangled analyses, no solutions, only the way to forgetting the self, the way to zazen, to "just sitting." Through zazen, ideas dissolve, the mind becomes transparent, and in the great stillness of samadhi, (Melville called it, "that profound silence, that only voice of God") there comes an intuitive understanding that what we seek lies nowhere else but in this present moment, *right here now where we have always been,* in the common miracle of our own divinity. To travel this path, one need not be a "Zen Buddhist"—call yourself a zazen Buddhist if you like! "Zen Buddhist" is only another idea to be discarded, like "enlightenment," or like "the Buddha," or like "God."

"Abide nowhere," says the *Diamond Sutra.* The

FOREWORD
Peter Ishin Matthiessen

last wish of the late Nyōgen Senzaki, a wonderful
Zen teacher of Los Angeles, was to leave no mark
of his passage through this life, but to blow away
into eternity, light as the dust of an old brown
mushroom in the woods.

XVI

Studies in Zen Buddhism tend to recount incomprehensible dialogues, or to create a picture of difficult asceticism. Something is missing, some organic link that can bring us ordinary people into a relationship with this important human tradition.

Somehow we sense that in those witty encounters between Zen personages and in those images of quiet sitting there may be a way for us to resolve the questions that waken us in the night,—What am I doing here? Where am I going?—and the like. But what a gulf there is between us fallible cowards and those enlightened masters and hard-bitten ascetics!

In reading John Daishin Buksbazen's *To Forget the Self* we learn how mistaken we have been in visualizing impossible states of mind and body. He has brought the practice home to us all. It is as simple as stretching exercises, as intimate as counting the breaths, as uncomplicated as accepting one's self, as ordinary as enjoying one's friends.

The way of Zen turns out to be a way to an end, certainly,—but there is no end. It is a way that is an end, fulfilled with each action of standing or speaking. *To Forget the Self* is a book that helps us to engage in such a way, step by step, with each step the very top.

It is fitting that it should be a part of the Zen Writings Series, as it presents the why, the how and the what of that practice. Daishin has brought his own warm humanity to an essentially human, deep concern.

We are very grateful to him.

PREFACE
Chōtan Aitken Roshi

Zen Buddhism, according to various authorities, is a religion, or a philosophy, or a way of life, or a mental/physical discipline. Some say it is all of the above; others say it is none.

Fundamentally, Zen is a way of seeing clearly who we are and what our life is, and a way of living based on that clear vision.

Many people wonder what Zen is all about, and how it works. They find much of the literature about Zen confusing and are unclear about how it applies to daily living.

This book is in large measure directed to those people. Its aim is to give enough information to get them started in Zen practice, especially in the form of seated meditation called *zazen,* or just *sitting.* The assumption is that this practice will do more for the inquiring individual than reading any number of books or articles. Once actual practice has begun, then books (carefully chosen for their relevance and reliability) can enrich and broaden one's understanding. But if there is not a sound foundation of experience, then the books will remain undigested in the domain of intellect, and not be of much use.

After all, cookbooks are fun to read, but they aren't very nutritious. They are most helpful to somebody who is actually involved in cooking.

So once you've read this book, the next step is to start practice. If your community has a Zen teacher, so much the better. If not, then you are on your own until you find one, and that is another of the concerns of this book. It is intended to give you enough information to get you started and keep you going until you can find and begin practice with a qualified teacher, either of Zen or of one of the related practices, such as Tibetan Buddhism.

Keep this in mind, though: sooner or later, you really must study with a teacher, for the practice is long and not easy, and there are numerous opportunities to become discouraged or confused along the way.

Also, as you progress you will have experiences to discuss and questions which should be reliably answered. This should be done on a personal basis by a qualified teacher who knows you and can deal with you directly. But this book can keep you going until you and your teacher meet.

Beyond looking at this book and thinking about it, there is another way to use it.

I've written it as conversationally as possible, so that you can imagine you're at a Zen center receiving the kind of introductory instruction commonly offered new sitters. One good way to use the book is to get together with a group of your friends who share your interest in practicing, and to take turns reading the instructions aloud while the entire group actually follows them step by step.

Somehow even though you may have read the words silently to yourself, they make more of an impact if you can also absorb them through the sense of hearing. Go slowly enough so that everyone in the group has plenty of time to follow each step. Pause often, and don't rush. Allow plenty of time to cover the material, and don't hesitate to repeat a section until it is clear to everyone. You'll often find that hearing a passage for the fifth or even the tenth time will give you new information.

If you're alone, you may find it helpful to make a cassette recording of these instructions, so that you can instruct yourself as you go. Recorded instructions are also available from the Zen Center of Los Angeles; please write for information about this resource.

The quotations in this book have been chosen because they enrich or enhance the text, and provide a counterpoint, often off-beat or humorous, to its principal themes. However, the fact that a particular author's statement bespeaks a realization similar to the one that arises in sitting does not in any way imply that, in general, he agrees with our point of view.

As for the photographic images of *To Forget the Self*, a word of introduction seems appropriate. For the most part, (except where otherwise noted), they are by John Daido Loori, and are rather more than simple illustrations. Arising as much in the unconscious of the reader as in the eye of the photographer, these images offer a space in which the mind's eye can freely roam, often leaving the conventions of documentary realism, yet rigorously meeting the requirements of clarified vision. They are to be explored rather than looked at; experienced rather than labeled. In them, one

INTRODUCTION

will find realities beyond the familiar, yet inseparable from the shapes and textures of our everyday life.

Finally, a word about the three sections into which this book is divided: "Buddhas," "Sitting," and "Community."

The first section deals with the experiences and teaching career of the historical Buddha, Shakyamuni, as well as briefly discussing the unbroken line of teachers who have been his successors through more than eighty generations down to the present day.

The second section focusses on sitting. It sets forth detailed instructions on how to do it, and places it in the context of an overall practice.

The third section extends those individual practices and discoveries to a larger community, providing the vital link between the individual and the society in which he or she exists.

By carefully reading all three sections, you will hopefully begin to get a sense of practice, and the way it functions in everyday life.

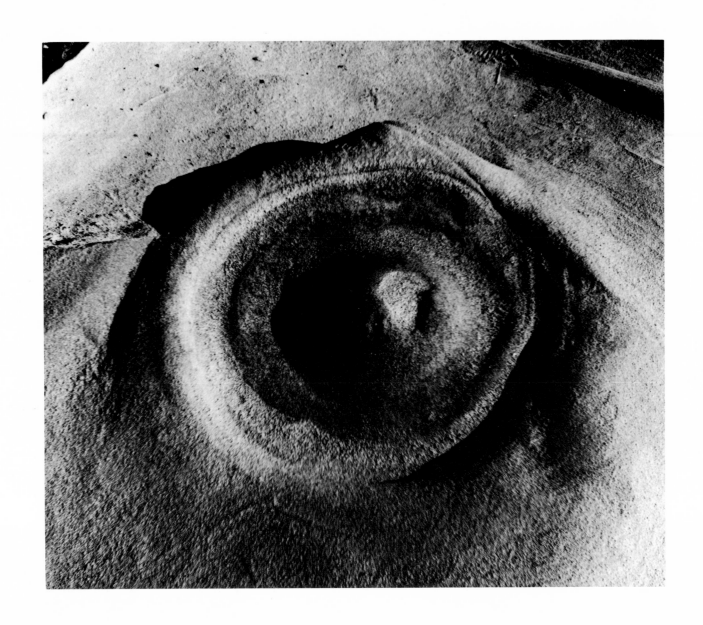

BUDDHAS

The Story of Shakyamuni Buddha

About twenty-five hundred years ago in India, the son of a wealthy and powerful nobleman made a profound discovery. Dissatisfied with his sheltered existence, and deeply troubled by the problems of life and death and human suffering all around him, he had left his family compound and set off upon a journey of self-exploration and study. And after many years of rigorous asceticism and scholarly philosophical research, he still had to admit that he was unable to answer the fundamental question, "What is life-and-death all about?"

At that point, he abandoned his previous practices of fasting, self-mortification and intellectual inquiry. He decided that the only way for him to really grapple with the question was directly to grapple with himself.

So he stopped fasting, bathed himself, had a bowl of milk (which really shocked his fellow-ascetics), and looked for the answer within himself. For six years, we are told, his main activity was to sit motionless hour after hour, looking deeply into his own mind. Now he knew he was on the right track; he could feel it as he grew steadier and stronger in his meditation. But even though he was really determined, it still took a lot of hard work for him not to become discouraged and not to wander off into some other activity.

But he kept at it steadily, and one day sensed that he was reaching a crisis. He simply *had* to break through whatever it was that separated him from realization of the Truth. And so it was,

in that frame of mind, that he sat down under a tree and vowed not rise until he had either answered his burning question or died in the attempt.

Sitting there, he focussed his whole attention upon that question, and became so absorbed in his consuming inquiry that he lost track of everything else. He didn't even think of himself or about the nature of the question; he was too busy questioning. He and the question no longer seemed to be two different things. It was as though he had totally become one with the question, had become the questioning itself.

On the morning of December eighth, as he sat there in deep meditation, he caught a glimpse of the morning star—the planet Venus—alone in the empty sky at dawn. And at that moment, something tremendous happened. He suddenly *was* that morning star, suddenly *was* the whole universe itself. Of course, this could have been precipitated by almost anything else: a chirping bird, a running dog, a stubbed toe. Almost any phenomenon could have triggered his breakthrough, once he had become sufficiently concentrated and focussed upon his question. But in the case of the man called Siddhartha Guatama, the stimulus was seeing the planet Venus. At that point, his question vanished, and he *knew*. It was as though he had suddenly awakened from a dream, and was able to see reality directly for the first time.

And from then on, people called him *Buddha*, which simply means "The One Who Woke Up."

2

Only that day dawns to which we are awake.
—Henry David Thoreau

3

The Lineage

He spent the rest of his life, nearly fifty years more, telling and showing people how they too could wake up by making the same discovery he had made. Gradually others came to practice sitting in meditation as he had taught, and found for themselves the experience of realizing who they truly were and what life and death were about on the most fundamental level.

Through the years following his breakthrough, many of his followers made the same discovery. But it was not until late in his career that the historical Buddha was satisfied that one of his disciples had really deepened and clarified his understanding sufficiently to carry on the teaching independently. Once he had found this person, a man named Maha Kasyapa, the Buddha publicly named him as the successor to his own understanding, to his own state of mind.

This man, Maha Kasyapa, in turn waited until he too could confidently name one of his disciples as successor, able to provide fully reliable instruction and guidance to future students.

And so it went, each successor in turn training many students and always looking for one or more of them who would have a deep and clear enough understanding and the right personal qualities to carry on the teaching.

This went on for twenty-eight generations in India, before one of these successors, Bodhidharma, finally found his way to China, bringing with him the practice of sitting. After six generations in China, the teaching spread to Korea, the rest of Asia, and eventually to Japan. What's really important to keep in mind about this continuation of the teachings is that it was never based upon purely intellectual or second-hand study; always the individuals who were entrusted with the responsibility to transmit Buddhism properly were those whose practice/ enlightenment were outstanding, and who had thoroughly grasped the essence of each phase of the teaching. Additionally, the personality of the individual especially suited him or her to the task. With these conditions satisfied, the person could then become a successor in the teaching lineage of his or her teacher.

It is this unbroken line of teachers and their successors which has helped ensure that the enlightenment of the historical Buddha continues through more than eighty generations from India through China to Japan and now to the Western world.

It is essential that one practice under the guidance of an authentic representative of this succession if one wishes to attain to a deep and clear understanding of life and death.

Buddhas in America

That Zen has been transmitted across culture and continents reminds us that Buddhism is not some alien Oriental mystery which we as Westerners cannot understand. It has come to us from the Orient, but the point is that we here in the West can now participate in this practice, not as foreigners dipping into an unfamiliar culture, but

4

in our own right, as ourselves, dipping into ourselves. When this takes place, Buddhism is as natural and indigenous to the West as those who practice it.

Today more than ever before we are concerned with the kinds of questions the Buddha was asking. We seem to be searching for some basic principle to tie everything together. We want this principle to be something which helps us to live and to grow harmoniously and sanely in an increasingly difficult world.

Being of a practical turn of mind, we don't want to settle for concepts alone, for vague emotional generalities, or to accept secondhand the insights of somebody else, no matter how revered or respected that other person might be. We want to find out for ourselves, directly, clearly, and without doubt, just who we are, what our life is, and what difference that makes.

In the day-to-day, month-to-month, year-to-year practice with a teacher who embodies that realization we find the inspiration and guidance that the students of Buddhism have always looked for from their teachers. And it is after this kind of training and realization that the student is ultimately weaned from his or her teacher, to take enlightenment itself as teacher and guide, having discovered who he or she really is, having forgotten the self.

Shakyamuni Buddha urged his students not to depend upon others, but to look to themselves for liberation. Seventeen centuries later, the great Japanese Zen master Dōgen taught:

A special transmission outside the scriptures,
No dependence on words and letters.
Seeing directly into the mind of man,
Realizing true nature, becoming Buddha.
—Bodhidharma, Zen master
(d. 532 A.D.)

To study the Buddha way is to study the self.
To study the self is to forget the self.

Here, in these pages, is how to get started doing just that.

Not equal to
Not metaphor
Not standing for
Not sign.
—Minor White

*What the Buddha had experienced was
. . . the direct and conscious realization of
the oneness of the whole universe and of his
own unity with all things. . . . To have
this very realization is in itself to be the
Buddha.*
—Taizan Maezumi Roshi

SITTING

The Nature of the Problem

When Shakyamuni Buddha first experienced enlightenment, he exclaimed that it was amazing, miraculous, and wonderful that all beings had the same wisdom and compassion as the fully-awakened one, but that since their perceptions were distorted they could not see this directly.

What he meant was that we tend to create a problem for ourselves by our accustomed way of thinking, and by the ingrained bias of our perceptions.

When we compulsively split ourselves and the world into pre-fabricated categories such as "good" and "bad," "us" and "them," "real" and "ideal," we get into serious difficulties.

It isn't so terrible to think logically and analytically; if we are designing a bridge or balancing a checkbook, that's the best way to think and be. But when you get right down to it, discursive, linear thinking is only useful for certain kinds of tasks, and for others it is quite useless. Like the hammer or the toothbrush, it is a tool intended for certain kinds of jobs. If you use a hammer to brush your teeth, or a toothbrush to drive nails, you are not likely to meet with great success.

The problem for most of us is that once we are born into this culture, we are very strongly conditioned and taught, from infancy onwards, to rely almost totally upon discursive logic and rational thought. We are generally discouraged from developing or relying on our innate ability to grasp reality intuitively or directly. Such abilities are labelled as "unscientific," and dismissed as "weird" or even "nonexistent." Even when

trying to deal with questions of ultimate values and purposes, when trying to approach ultimate reality, we are urged to remain in the modes of thought learned in elementary school classes, and not to entrust ourselves to other ways of knowing reality.

So it is that we are indoctrinated to disown and to lose contact with an extremely important aspect of ourselves, and to rely compulsively and inappropriately on another. As a result, we are forever separating from ourselves, stepping back a few paces, and looking at, rather than being, who we are.

And as we do that, we create a split or a gap which we experience as alienation, or loneliness, or boredom, or frustration, or craving, or revulsion. We see ourselves as individual "selves" encased in skinprisons and doomed to perpetual solitary confinement. Of course, we have such a wonderful assortment of entertainments and pastimes in prison that we manage to divert ourselves from that wan awareness much of the time. But sooner or later in most lives there comes a time when the individual senses, more or less painfully, that something is fundamentally *not quite right*. Our tendency is then to look for the sources of the problem in social, political, economic or interpersonal terms. Even when in traditional Western psychology we "turn inwards," we generally choose to deal with our memories and feelings in terms of interactions with others, seeing ourselves as acted-upon and at least partially determined by forces outside our control.

Because there is some truth to these perspectives, we cling to them stubbornly, knowing ourselves and our worlds only through a thick filter of theories and analytical reasoning. Many never go further than this. But a growing number of us are finding this approach to understanding life ultimately unsatisfying, inadequate to deal with truly fundamental questions.

At this point, we begin to look for a more radical approach, one which goes to the roots of existence, rather than remaining focussed on the leaves and branches of the tree of life.

The Nature of the Solution

Sitting is just such an approach, a way of getting deeply in touch with the *Self*. Not just with the *self*; that much can be accomplished through psychotherapy or a number of other disciplines. But sitting deals with the "big-S" Self, that most basic level of reality which has nothing to do with culture, social status, intellect or even personality. It deals with who you really are *beyond* all these considerations of time and place. And who you really are is ultimately the universe itself.

But sitting is also much more than a method of experiencing the Self in this way. It's also a direct expression of what it was that Shakyamuni Buddha found out. Of what it is that you, the buddha, find out. That's why you'll discover that sitting is not only a tool, a means toward an end, but that it is also a way of life which is a living model of living itself.

I exist as I am, that is enough,
If no other in the world be aware
I sit content,
And if each and all be aware I sit content.
—Walt Whitman

Starting to Sit

When you begin to sit, it is best not to try too much right away. If you begin by sitting about fifteen minutes a day, that's enough; you'll be less likely to wear yourself out or get discouraged that way. Build up your sitting time very gradually, perhaps a minute longer every few days, until you can sit reasonably well for about a half-hour at a time.

And remember, it's not nearly as important how *long* you sit, as it is how *regularly* and *vigorously* you sit, and how carefully you follow these instructions.

It's much better to sit hard every day for a half-hour or so than to sit for an hour or two several times a month.

Sitting hard simply means that even when you don't feel particularly enthusiastic or in the mood for sitting, you still sit down and do your level best. Even if you have a rough time of it, you can be sure that that kind of sincere effort will be quite effective.

In fact, you are likely to find out gradually that not only are all those "problems" you encounter in trying to sit well quite natural, but also that your very dealing with those "problems" is, in itself, the life of your sitting practice. I put the word "problems" in quotes, because I keep finding that difficulties only become problems when I separate myself from them instead of dealing with them directly and wholeheartedly. So don't worry if your sitting doesn't come easily —just view everything as a helpful lesson, take everything as it comes, *without comment*, and you'll do well.

Some Rules-of-Thumb

When you begin to sit, you need to be quite careful about how you arrange your legs, how your spine is adjusted and other seemingly unimportant details. It's like laying the foundation for a building—if the foundation is not level and properly lined up, the whole building will be shaky. So even if you have a little trouble getting the position right, be patient and careful with yourself, so that you can get settled into a good posture for sitting.

In the appendix on exercises, several suggestions are made to help you limber up. But whatever you do, don't go to extremes. Sitting isn't meant to be a form of self-torture or punishment! Nor is it meant to be practiced casually at irregular intervals. Just work at it daily for a moderate length of time, and let your practice grow at a natural pace.

Here are some *rules-of-thumb* to follow when sitting:

1. When you sit, try to make your body into a tripod or pyramid shape by making a three-pointed base of your two knees and your buttocks. Except when you sit in a chair, both knees should stay in contact with the floor at all times when sitting.

2. Once you've gotten seated, your spine should be erect, not stiffly as in a military brace position, but not slumped over into an exaggerated "S" curve either.

3. Your torso should be perpendicular to the floor, not leaning to the right or left, or forward or backward. The same thing applies to your head; it should rest squarely atop your spine,

The practice must be engaged, it must be entered. You must realize by action. In other words, not up in the head or only by concentration, but all together with the body.
—Taizan Maezumi Roshi

and not tilt in any direction.

4. Wear loose, baggy clothes when sitting, so you don't cut off your circulation or constrict the breathing movement of your rib cage or lower belly muscles.

One last note, before you get started. In sitting, two items of equipment are recommended: a pill-shaped cushion called a *zafu,* and a thick rectangular mat called a *zabuton.* Either or both of these can be purchased by mail from ZCLA, or if you'd like to make your own, see Appendix II of this book. And if you want, you can even fold up a couple of army blankets to make a reasonable substitute for these two items. The only thing to keep in mind about cushions is that you should avoid foam rubber or other synthetics because they tend to lack the firmness of kapok, and will give you a wobbly seat.

When you sit, your zafu goes on top of the zabuton, and you go on top of the zafu. But don't try to sit squarely in the middle of the zafu; rather use it as a kind of wedge under your buttocks, using only the forward third of the zafu to actually support you. This will help you place the weight of your body more toward a central area between the three points of your tripod-base, and relieve some strain on your spinal column.

Now let's look at the various positions in which you can sit. Try them all out, and pick the one which works best for you *at your present stage of development.* Don't try to force your legs into the full- or half-lotus if they really just won't go.

There's no value in hurting yourself. Zazen, in fact, should be comfortable.

Positioning the Legs

In order of difficulty, the sitting positions are:
the *full-lotus* position
   (this one's the toughest but the best);
the *half-lotus* position
   (almost as good, and a little easier);
the *burmese* position
   (not quite as good, but lots easier);
seiza or *kneeling* position
   (quite easy for most folks);
chair sitting (especially recommended for sitters who, because of age, illness, or physical condition cannot sit in any of the above positions.)

In setting out directions for sitting in these positions, we'll first describe in some detail the arrangement of the legs. Once your legs are arranged in the position you've decided to use, the rest of the instructions pretty much apply equally to all the positions.

The Full-Lotus

The *full-lotus* position is the best way to sit for a number of reasons. It offers the most stable and symmetrical position in general, and specifically gives the spine the most support. In the long run, it is also the most comfortable of all the positions, once you get used to sitting that way. And of course, that's the main difficulty. Getting into this position and getting used to it are often too tough for new sitters, who find their legs hurt so badly that they just can't make this position at all. This is mostly due to the tightness of your leg muscles. With steady practice, you'll loosen up considerably.

If at first you can't get into the full-lotus position, don't push yourself, for there is a real chance of hurting yourself if you go too far too fast. A general rule is: *do it if you have only mild discomfort, but don't do it if you have severe pain.*

Once you've seated yourself upon the zafu, place your right foot on your left thigh, and the left foot on the right (or vice-versa if more comfortable.) Make sure your heels are drawn up as close to your abdomen as possible, rather than letting your feet slip down towards the inside of the thighs or the calves. In this position, the soles of both your feet should tend to point at the ceiling. If at all possible, the toes of both feet should project freely beyond the thigh, so that they can be wiggled without encountering any resistance.

The Half-Lotus Position

This position is basically the same as the full-lotus, except that the right foot is tucked under the left thigh and rests upon the floor (or the zabuton if you're using one,) while the left foot goes on top of the right thigh. This position is usually easier than the full-lotus to get into when you're first starting out, since less pressure is put on the knees and legs. The disadvantage, however, is that this position isn't as balanced as the

Even monkeys fall out of trees.
—Japanese proverb

17

full-lotus, since one foot is up on the thigh and the other is under the thigh on the ground. The result is a tendency for your body to tilt slightly to one side, which must be compensated for very carefully when you get into the position. This compensation happens when you reach the stage of swaying (see page 23). Also, your left knee will tend to rise into the air, and you'll have to use a higher zafu so that both knees rest solidly upon the floor or zabuton. Generally speaking, the further you go from the full-lotus, the higher your zafu should be. (Naturally, this doesn't apply to sitting in a chair or in the kneeling position.) Finally, since your pelvis isn't as well-supported in this position, it'll be easier for your back to slump and curve, thus spoiling your posture. But if you're aware of these difficulties and make the necessary adjustments, you'll find the *half-lotus* to be a very effective sitting position, and one which will help you get ready for the full-lotus as time goes by. In order to make this position even more of a help, try reversing your legs every other time you sit; that is, instead of having the left foot up and the right foot under, put the right foot up and the left under. That will increase flexibility in both legs, and be a big help to you.

The Burmese Position

In the Burmese position, draw the right foot up close to the left thigh (or vice-versa), allowing the foot and calf to rest on the floor or zabuton. Then place the left foot in front of the right calf so that both knees touch the mat. If your knees don't reach the mat, try using a higher zafu, and if this doesn't help, you might consider placing support cushions under your knees.

Usually, this position is much easier to get into than either full- or half-lotus positions. It certainly is a lot easier on the legs. But because it really doesn't do much to support your pelvis and spine in the proper alignment, it tends to be most tiring to the back over a long period of time. Nonetheless, it's a good position for beginners, and even experienced sitters find that they can do good sitting in the Burmese position.

You just have to be more careful with your back, and be alert for the first signs that your posture is beginning to slump so that you can correct it.

Also remember that this position requires the highest zafu of all the positions. Some folks just put one zafu on top of another, and that's okay to do. But watch your back. If if doesn't hurt when you sit for a half-hour, fine. But if you get back pains or stiffness, then you need to correct your posture.

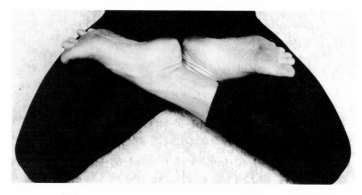

The full-lotus position

When we have our body and mind in order, everything else will exist in the right place, in the right way.
—Shunryu Suzuki Roshi
(1904-1971)

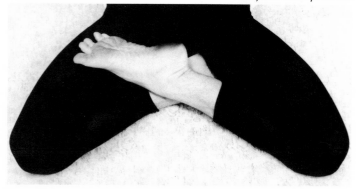

The half-lotus position

The Burmese position

The Seiza or Kneeling Position

To do this one, kneel with the zafu on edge between your heels (see photo). Then sit back, as though to sit on your heels, and let the zafu bear the weight of your body. Remember that the basic model is the tripod or pyramid, so keep your knees far enough apart to give you a steady base. Otherwise this posture will be hard to maintain, and you'll wobble around a lot, which is not helpful to your sitting or concentration.

Lots of times it helps, especially if you're sitting more than one period, to alternate positions from one period to the next. That way you spread the stress more evenly, and your legs won't get quite as tired as if you sit in only one position.

Sitting in a Chair

Somehow people seem to feel reluctant about sitting in a chair, as though it were less authentic or spiritual to do it that way than with legs crossed on the floor.

Actually, even though chair sitting has its own problems, there is no reason why you can't sit very well in a chair, either temporarily until you get in shape for floor sitting, or permanently if your age, physique, or condition require it.

As in other positions, the important thing is to get your posture perpendicular to the floor and to straighten the spine.

The tough part about chair-sitting is that it's super-easy to slump, then slouch, and finally collapse against the chair-back. And that's not good.

The best chair to use is a plain, unupholstered wooden kitchen chair. Also good to use is a simple piano bench or stool without a back. Just place your zafu on the seat of the chair or bench.

Sit on the forward third of the zafu, so that your back is not touching the back of the chair and your knees are slightly lower than your hips. This frees the abdomen, and encourages unrestricted breathing. Next, place your feet squarely on the floor, about the same distance apart as your shoulders. Let your hands rest upon your thighs in the position shown in the illustration.

The kneeling position

Sitting in a chair

Positioning the Body

By now you've learned about how the legs are arranged in all of the five sitting positions. From here on, instructions for positioning your body are the same no matter how you are sitting.

Spine

Once you have taken a position and arranged your legs, the next step is to center your spine.

Imagine that your spine is a pendulum, hinged at the tailbone, and with your head at the top end as the weight. Swaying in large arcs, move your torso and abdomen first to the left, then right, then left, etc., as though you were a metronome. Don't let your head move independently, but just make it an extension of your spine, so the air passage from head to body is always aligned and clear from obstruction. And when swaying, always keep your knees firmly planted on the floor or zabuton (except, of course, when sitting in a chair.)

Start in a wide arc, and feel the pull of gravity as you reach the outside point of that arc. Sway slowly enough to feel that tug—no use hurrying, take your time. Notice how it seems to decrease as you straighten back up? And when you're in an upright position (perpendicular to the floor), notice that there's practically no sense of pull. Then as you sway over to the other side, notice that pulling sensation return.

Now let the size of the arcs naturally decrease as your momentum dies down, until you just drift to a stop. If you can keep from controlling

When you sit, your breath and body and mind become harmonized, and when your breath slows down, the mind also calms down. So try to have this unified, comfortable feeling when you do zazen, and please do not be hasty. . . . Each of you has to find the suitable, comfortable way to achieve this unified, harmonized condition of breathing, body and mind.
—Kōryū Ōsaka Roshi

21

the rate of speed and the duration of the swings, you will have become a natural plumb-bob, and will come to rest in a position which is perpendicular to the floor. This will center you properly so that you don't lean in any particular direction, but are sitting straight. Of course, if you try to speed up or slow down deliberately, what you're actually doing is fighting the laws of gravity and momentum, and you're more likely to wind up sitting crookedly or leaning that way. As always, if you can just harmonize with the laws of nature, you avoid creating problems.

Next step is to straighten your back. Now normally the spine has a certain degree of curvature to it, and this isn't a problem in itself. You shouldn't try to make your spine ramrod-straight like an iron bar or a yardstick. Not only is that contrary to how human beings are built, but it would probably tend to give you back trouble over time.

Your main concern now is to let your spine be in the best natural position possible. In that position, your vertebrae aren't all compressed and squashed down upon one another, and you aren't pinching nerves or assuming the posture of exaggerated spinal curvature called lordosis. Here's how to get your back straightened properly.

Imagine that the ceiling is resting on the crown of your head at a point directly over your spine. Now imagine that you are going to act as a jack, and that your spine is going to push the ceiling up a little bit. But the action is all in your spine,

so be careful not to tense your shoulders or move your head. Just let your spine begin to extend itself, from the base of the spine upwards toward the head, carrying the head with it as it straightens. Feel the thrust move upwards from the tailbone, and notice that as you do so, there's a tendency to stick your belly out and to let your buttocks protrude backwards a bit, as if you were doing a kind of dance.

Now let the energy flow upward, and as you do so, lift that ceiling a half-inch. Don't tilt your head backwards or forwards, though. Let your spine do the lifting. Push harder. Harder still. Harder.

And now relax.

Notice that you stayed erect? That when you relaxed there was no cave-in? That's because you first seated yourself carefully and then centered your spine before you tried to straighten up. If you did all those things quite carefully, according to the instructions, you found that it wasn't necessary after all to use a lot of muscular effort to sit upright and to stay there. Sitting straight and tall and erect is mostly a matter of getting arranged properly, rather than a tug-of-war against gravity.

It's like balancing a bamboo pole on its end; if the pole is perpendicular to the ground, it will remain upright as long as nothing else acts to pull it over. But if the pole is even *slightly* crooked or out of plumb, it will tend to fall over in that direction unless you reach out and grab it to keep it from falling.

Our bodies are also subject to the same law of gravity as that pole. Keeping upright is only an effort if you're using your back muscles to keep you erect by brute force; that is, if you are constantly "reaching out and grabbing" yourself to keep from toppling over, slowly and majestically like a felled pine. Your back muscles function like retro-rockets on a spacecraft; they are designed to work for only short periods of time, and in short bursts of effort to make minor course corrections. That's all they can really do. If we demand of them that they keep us upright steadily for a long time, such as ten or twenty minutes or longer, we are asking too much. Of course, the muscles will obediently try to do so, but will get so fatigued after just a short time that a backache will occur. If you don't heed that warning signal, then muscle spasms and more severe back trouble may result.

In general, back pain is a signal that you aren't sitting quite straight. If you correct your position (by doing the ceiling-pushing-up exercise) you'll generally find the back pain going away. Always pay attention to back pain or discomfort when sitting. Unlike leg discomfort, back pain *is* significant and should be heeded.

Remember, all these techniques are primarily intended to help you find and keep a comfortable, balanced posture.

Head and Hands

Having arranged your legs in one of the basic positions, and having centered and straightened your back, the next step is to arrange your head and hands.

This is not very difficult. Since your head is already attached to the end of your spine, you simply allow it to remain there without interference! This means that your head, positioned in line with your spine, should not lean either forward or backwards, or to either side. Your ears should be parallel with your shoulders, and the tip of your nose roughly centered over your navel. Tuck your chin in just a little bit, and close your mouth. Now place the tip of your tongue against the roof of your mouth, just behind the front teeth. Swallow your saliva, and evacuate some of the air from your mouth, so that there is a slight vacuum. This will slow down your salivation rate so you won't have to keep swallowing saliva as often as you normally would.

Your eyes should be lowered to approximately a 45-degree angle, neither fully open nor closed, but just half-opened and gazing in the direction of the floor about three or four feet ahead of you. (If you're facing the wall and it's closer than three or four feet from you, pretend to be looking through the wall at where the floor would be.) With the eyes in this position, you won't have to blink very often, and you will find that fewer things distract you visually. Generally you're better off not closing your eyes completely,

because that tends to make you feel drowsy.

Finally, your hands should be arranged in a special way called a *mudra*. The most common one is called the *cosmic mudra,* and is formed as follows:

Place your right hand, palm up, so that the blade of the hand (the part you would strike with in a karate chop) rests against your lower belly. Then place the left hand, palm upwards also, on top of the right, so that the middle knuckles overlap and the thumb-tips lightly touch, forming an oval frame.

The positioning of the thumb-tips is important, for if your attention wanders, you'll find that the thumbs move apart. And if your sitting has become dull and drowsy, you'll usually find that the thumbs sag in the middle, showing the loss of alertness. So the thumbs can serve you well as a built-in biofeedback device, to continuously reflect the state of your mind.

Another point often discussed is the placement of the hands relative to the rest of the body. If you are sitting in the full lotus position, the heels form a natural base to support the backs of your hands, so that's no problem. But if you are sitting in one of the other positions, you may find that your hands are not symmetrically arranged or that your arms and shoulders get sore from the strain of supporting the hands (which are a little bit on the heavy side) for a full period of sitting. So rather than straining to place your hands in some idealized position, simply let them rest naturally in your lap, as close to the ideal position shown in these photographs as you can get. But don't let your hand position get to be a distraction for you.

When your body is in position for sitting, run down this checklist to make sure everything is arranged properly:

1. Sit on the forward third of your zafu.

2. Arrange your legs in the position you can do best.

3. Sway in decreasing arcs to center your spine.

4. Straighten your spine and align your head by doing the ceiling-pushing-up exercise.

5. Lower your eyes and allow them to go out of focus.

6. Close your mouth and position your tongue.

7. Place your hands in the cosmic mudra.

8. Make sure your whole body is arranged the way you want it before you begin sitting.

Zazen is not a difficult task. It is a way to lead you into your long-lost home.
—Soyen Shaku, Zen master (1859-1919)

Always remember this rule of thumb: Except for the normal discomfort always associated with a new kind of physical activity, zazen should be comfortable, not agonizing. All of these instructions are intended primarily to help you get and stay comfortable in your sitting. Don't get involved in a competition with yourself or anyone else just to see how much you can take. Be strong and calm, and pay close attention to what you are doing. Little else is as important as the attitude of the sitter.

Breathing

All life depends on breathing, and yet few people really know how to breathe. They are so used to surviving with the breathing habits of the average person, that they mistake the familiarity of breathing with being able to do it well. But what passes for breathing in most folks is more often a kind of panting or gasping.

You've probably noticed that when you run up a couple of flights of stairs or chase a bus, you breathe very heavily, with your chest heaving up and down as you attempt to get enough oxygen. This is obvious panting, and nobody is surprised by it. But when you are sitting still, not straining every muscle for some heavy physical task, there is no real need to continue breathing as though you were running up stairs.

If you are average in your breathing habits, you probably breathe about fifteen to eighteen breath-cycles per minute *when at rest*. This is called your basic breathing rate. It is so common

a breathing rate that it is easy to get used to it and to regard it as natural, as though it were the result of how you were constructed in the first place.

But it isn't so.

If you don't fight yourself with poor posture, cramped muscles and internal organs, and an over-active forebrain, you'll find that your breathing will change. It will slow down and become smooth and rhythmic until you are breathing at perhaps five or fewer breath-cycles per minute. And it will do so more effectively if you do not strain or struggle to control your breath.

You don't really need to breathe any more than that when sitting; you're just used to panting because you've had to all your life, due to improper posture. But when you start sitting regularly, you will really get in touch with the breathing process which maintains your life.

Needless to say, in the profound stillness of zazen, the constant struggle for oxygen is a loud and disturbing whirlwind of activity which helps protect us from the much-feared stillness. In this way we avoid ourselves without consciously trying to do so.

Breathing in Zazen

Once you have allowed your body to sit, you must allow your breath to sit as well. Having reached a centered and balanced position, with legs and hands arranged correctly, and with your spine erect, take a few deep breaths and release

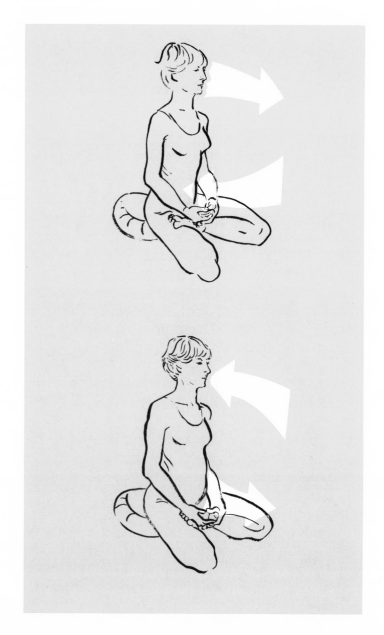

What we call 'I' is just a swinging door which moves when we inhale and when we exhale. . . . When your mind is pure and calm enough to follow this movement, there is nothing: no 'I', no world, no mind nor body; just a swinging door.
—Shunryu Suzuki Roshi

them, inhaling through the mouth and exhaling through the nose. These first few breaths will clear your lungs and oxygenate your blood, and will give you a fresh supply of air with which to start.

Forget about trying to control the flow of air in and out of your body, and just concentrate on being aware of what your breath is doing. Is is fast? That's okay. Is it slow? That's fine. Deep? Great. Shallow? No problem. Just watch what's happening with your breathing and don't try to make corrections right away. Keep breathing through your nose the way your body tells you to, and let yourself be very clearly aware of all the sensations which accompany the flow of breath in and out of your body.

When you've done this a few minutes, you'll notice that your upper body and trunk are relaxed and that your breathing has begun to assert its own natural speed and rhythm. When this has happened, you are ready to start regulating the breath.

Focussing your attention in the area of the lower belly, imagine that there's a balloon down there, and that each time you inhale, you're inflating that balloon. Then, as you exhale, imagine that balloon being deflated. Forget about your lungs, chest, and upper torso. They'll take care of themselves. Just concentrate on inflating and deflating that balloon, but at the same time, don't be too forceful about it. You're not trying to burst the balloon, just inflate it!

Feel the air move into that balloon, and feel the walls of the balloon bulge outwards as the balloon is slowly and steadily inflated. Now let the balloon start to contract inwards, as the air moves out of it and through your air passages to be exhaled from the nose. Feel that movement of the abdominal wall? Keep it steady now. If you're having trouble getting the feel of your lower belly muscles, see the appendix on exercises, page 64, and do the exercise called "lifting the weight." Then go back to sitting while the memory of how that felt is still fresh in your mind.

Proper breathing involves two basic types of muscular movement: horizontal and vertical.

The diaphragm moves vertically, and the wall of the lower belly moves horizontally.

The diaphragm is a thick, muscular membrane stretched across the body a little above the midsection. As the diaphragm moves up and down, it alternately pulls air into and pushes air out of the lungs.

At the same time that the diaphragm is moving vertically, the wall of the lower belly swells out slightly. Then as exhalation takes place, the belly wall moves back, and actually sinks into the abdomen as the diaphragm moves back up.

To really practice this kind of natural breathing, remember to avoid tight clothing, especially at the waist or chest, so that your breathing movements are not constricted. And also try to avoid eating just before you sit. If your stomach is full of food, it's likely to get in the way of your diaphragm and thus interfere with your breathing.

Actually, that's all there is to it—relaxed yet watchful breathing through the nose and letting the lower belly wall expand with each inhalation and contract with each exhalation. That's all there is to breathing. And yet, what a lot is contained within that seemingly simple process.

Imagine that you are making a graph of your breathing. Your "normal" (i.e., usual) breathing might look like a stock-market graph, with jagged straight lines connecting peaks and valleys, and with steep slopes to show the linear in/out, on/off patterns we've gotten used to over the years.

Now imagine a graph of someone sitting in zazen. Right away we can see that the frequency of breathing is reduced, until it goes from approximately fifteen breath-cycles per minute to around four or five breath-cycles per minute.

Note also that the transition from exhaling to inhaling and back again is less definite in zazen breathing than in common "normal" breathing patterns. On our imaginary graph, the lines change from sharp peaks and valleys with steep slopes, like so:

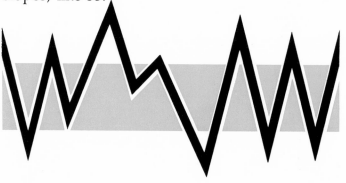

Even though waves arise, the essence of your mind is pure; it is just like clear water with a few waves. Actually water always has waves. Waves are the practice of the water.
—Shunryu Suzuki Roshi

29

to gentle curves, like so:

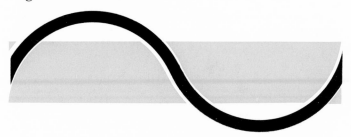

That's what it means to regulate the breath. You simply get out of your own way, and allow your body to function naturally. You don't have to be "in control." Marvelously equipped as we are, the process takes care of itself. All you have to do is to sit in the proper position, and then relax. Then you can recognize that you yourself *are* the process of breathing, and nothing extra in the way of gimmicks or techniques is necessary.

When this process gets comfortable and regular, you are ready to attend to the third aspect of zazen practice: regulating the activity of the mind.

Regulating the Mind

In some ways, the mind is very much like a pond or a lake. When the water is still and nothing is stirring, the surface of the water becomes smooth as glass, and clearly reflects the moon overhead in sharp detail.

But if the water is stirred up, waves and ripples mar the reflecting surface, and the clear moon becomes distorted until only glimmers of shattered light can be seen. Not until the disturbance dies down can you once again see the reflection of reality in its fullness and without distortion.

When you seat yourself properly, you are stilling some of the biggest, most obvious waves, those brought about by physical movement. That's why it's important to sit still and not fidget. If your body is motionless, you won't create a heavy flow of physical sensations which stir up big waves.

Going a step further, when you learn to breathe well, you calm the surface of the pond still more, and bring yourself that much closer to the mirror state.

But you are still far from mirror-like reflection as long as your mind is stirred up by fantasies and daydreams, discursive thinking, and all the many forms of ungoverned mental activity that seem to go on endlessly most of the time.

Most of the time you carry a heavy burden—the thick screen of self-consciousness through which everything is filtered. Most of the time, this self-consciousness is so familiar that you don't notice it. But every once in a while, especially if you're trying to sit, you find yourself suddenly very much aware of it. A lot of what goes on is a matter of continuously evaluating and commenting on whatever captures your attention. It can really get noticeable if you haven't been practicing zazen, and need for some reason to just sit still.

Let's say, for example, that you are sitting quietly in a room, not doing much of anything, just sitting there passing the time. How often do you shift your position in the chair? How many day-dreams are born and flourish in the silence of the crowded empty room? A fire engine races by outside. Instead of simply hearing it and letting it go, isn't it more usual to comment on the sound? ("Why *must* those damn fire engines keep going past *my* door?") Or perhaps you enter into an entire fantasy about it:

"I wonder where the fire is? Maybe it's that empty house on the corner, what a firetrap, what do the owners expect to happen if a fire breaks out there some day . . . maybe today is that day after all, oh lord, that's no kind of thought to be thinking, to wish the fire to happen to prove a point just because I don't approve of absentee landlords . . . of course that's always been a problem in and of itself, the problem of the landlord who, because he doesn't have to live there himself, is not confronted with the physical condition of his property on a daily basis, so he feels free to let it get run down and fall apart until a fire comes along and destroys the building . . . poetic justice, that, except that the poor tenants are the ones who are left homeless and who have to put up with the miserable conditions day after day until the fire happens to bring matters to a head. . . ."

It's almost funny when you consider it care-fully: on the one hand, we just hate to do with-out all those entertaining ripples and waves in

"The time has come," the Walrus said,
"To talk of many things:
Of shoes—and ships—and sealing wax
Of cabbages—and kings—
And why the sea is boiling hot
And whether pigs have wings."
—Lewis Carroll

31

the surface of the pond, and on the other, we feel the deep need for some basic silence and clarity so that we can see without the distortions and confusion caused by the very same ripples and waves we created in the first place!

Somehow it's really hard to sit still and stay alert and attentive without a lot of thinking or entertainment going on.

It's not terribly difficult to concentrate on an exciting movie, for it offers many crutches to support weak concentration from moment to moment. If a particular moment in the movie isn't interesting, that's okay because in the very next moment something else may come along to claim attention. All you have to do is to sit back passively and let the images wash over you. Moment after moment, something always comes along to rescue you from boredom, without any real effort on your part. ("*Wow! Look at that ripple!*") And generally those boredom-avoiding attention-grabbers are brightly-colored, loud, boisterous, and flashy, so that even the most superficial attention will yield a rich harvest of sensory stimuli and highly entertaining mental responses. In this way the pond is kept stirred up continuously, and you manage to keep yourself out of touch with your true nature.

So your first job in regulating your mind is to get your mind to sit along with your body and breath. You do this by counting your breaths:

First, seat yourself properly and allow your breathing to become regular and calm.

As you start to exhale, count that exhalation as the number *one*. Then, when you inhale, count that inhalation as *two*. Then as you exhale again, count that as *three*, and the following inhalation as *four*, and so on until you reach *ten*. Then start all over again on the very next breath with the number *one*, and repeat the counting from *one* through *ten*, over and over again. Keep doing this steadily until you can do it with full attention, not losing count, getting bored, daydreaming, or in any way interrupting your concentration.

This is a very *simple* thing to do, but it's not easy. One thing that most people have trouble with when starting out is that they keep thinking thoughts, and find this distressing. To put this in perspective, let's take a look at the two kinds of thinking which concern us.

First of all, since the nature of the human brain is to generate thoughts continuously, nobody need feel upset by that fact. As long as you are not unconscious or brain-damaged, you will produce one thought after another. This is quite normal.

These innocent flashes of mental activity called *random thoughts* are not a problem in sitting, for they are simply the natural action of a healthy brain. If you tried to stop those random thoughts you would have a very hard time, and would go into a kind of trance-state which is not at all what zazen is about. You are not trying to stop all thoughts from occurring.

On the other hand, there is a kind of thinking which is precisely what you must not encourage when you sit, for it will then dominate your mind as it already has all of your life. That form of thought is called *discursive thought*, or *linear thought*, for it consists of a progression of ideas, arising originally from a spontaneous and random thought, and gradually turning into an elaborate theatrical or philosophical production which takes you quite effectively out of your concentration and stirs up the surface of the water.

But to deal with either random thoughts or discursive thoughts, the procedure is the same. As soon as you realize what is happening, stop, go back to *one*, and start counting again with renewed vigor. If you only have random thoughts from time to time, you can just keep on going and ignore them. But if the random thoughts start turning into stream-of-consciousness soliloquies, then you must immediately return to *one* and start your counting again.

The principle involved is basically quite simple; it is the fact that nobody can really concentrate on two things at once. If this seems to be happening, in reality neither thought-object is getting your full attention. And conversely, if you really turn your attention wholly onto one focal point, there's no attention left over for such thoughts as distraction, boredom, or neurotic patterns of thought.

Don't be fooled by the simplicity of this exercise. It may take quite a bit of hard work until you can even count once from *one* to *ten*. If you don't consciously keep your attention strong, it'll

All thoughts of a turtle are turtle.
—Ralph Waldo Emerson

fade out by itself, and you'll have to go back to *one* all over again and start out fresh. And remember—no cheating! Even if you remember what number you were on when you lost count or started daydreaming, you *must* go back to *one* and start again. That way, you'll soon develop strong concentration, and the results will encourage you to go further. This is a lot like lifting weights. Even if you're weak when you start, regular workouts will soon produce results.

Up until now, we've spoken about the three aspects of sitting—body, breath and mind—in separate sections, but in actual practice, you'll be working on all three all the time. In fact, body, breath and mind are inseparable. The better your posture, the more well-aligned you can make your spine, the easier your breathing will become and the quieter your mind will be. And on the other hand, the clearer your mind and the stronger your concentration, the less difficulty you will have keeping your back straight, or sitting through your discomforts without fidgeting or changing position.

With this in mind, don't be discouraged if, for example, your posture doesn't come along as quickly as your breathing. Each person's practice develops differently, and usually the three aspects of sitting will mature at different rates.

Here again, the need for a personal teacher-student relationship is likely to make itself felt. As you practice this sitting sincerely and energetically, you are likely to encounter experiences and questions which are important to resolve.

No book could ever deal effectively with all the possible experiences, since they always arise intimately out of the depths of who you are. In the course of practice, then, it is really important to have access to a qualified teacher in whom you can trust and with whom you can honestly discuss your practice. If you follow the instructions in this book carefully, though, you will have gotten a good start on basic practice, and that should sustain you until you are ready to find your teacher in person.

*If the doors of perception were cleansed,
every thing would appear to man as it is,
infinite.*
—William Blake

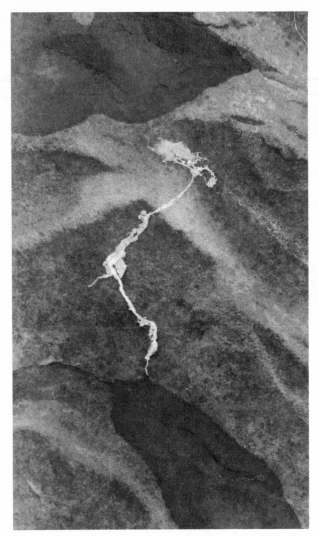

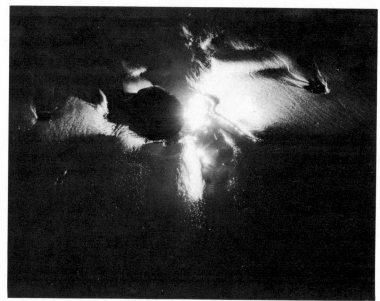

. . . music heard so deeply
That it is not heard at all, but you are the
music.
—T.S. Eliot

COMMUNITY

What Is Community?

So far, everything described could be practiced by a solitary individual. But true Zen practice cannot be fully experienced in all its diversity and richness by just one person. Sooner or later it becomes necessary to join with a group of people who together form a community of practice.

That practice comes out of each person's determination to achieve some deep, fundamental understanding of what this life really means, what this self really is.

If a *buddha* is one who realizes and lives enlightenment, and *sitting* is the deepest expression of that realization and life, then *community* is nothing other than going deeper and deeper into that realization, and becoming more and more at one with that life.

This seems to happen most readily and most fully when we are doing it in the company of others who are also doing the same thing.

Practicing together like this, we are in harmony with all sorts of situations, with all beings and with all conditions, as well as with the many facets of our own selves.

Being in harmony, though, does not necessarily imply a state of unbroken sweetness and light. *Rather, it suggests a readiness to deal appropriately with all events and circumstances without becoming separate or alienated from either oneself or one's surroundings.* It is a harmony based on this single, clear realization: that *everything*, you, me, the whole universe *as is* is one. And being one,

there is nothing "else" with which to conflict. *I can only be at odds with myself.*

Of course, that doesn't imply a passive acceptance of events or conditions. Members of the community work together and as individuals to take care of everything in the best way possible. When sick, we seek proper medical care; when hungry, we feed ourselves.

Neither does it imply that differences do not exist, nor that the community is free of disagreements or frictions. It's just that we try to remember that such situations are occasions for us to practice, to experience, and then to let go of our limited point of view.

What it *does* mean is that between subject and object there is no gap; that problems tend to contain within themselves their causes and their solutions.

And when we view things from this non-dualistic perspective, we can see a very special, and at the same time very ordinary, harmony everywhere, always.

Group Practice

Group practice in a Zen community usually takes one or more of three basic forms: daily practice, training period, and sesshin.

Daily Practice

First of all, there is the day-to-day practice schedule, which differs from place to place. It usually combines several hours of daily sitting with meals, work-practice, and chanting according to a regular timetable. For example this is a typical day's schedule at the Zen Center of Los Angeles:

Mornings	4:30	Wake-up
	5:00	Sitting (two 35-minute periods with walking meditation in between)
	6:30	chanting
	7:00	exercise or study
	8:00	breakfast
	8:45	work-practice
Afternoons	12:15	clean up
	12:30	chanting
	12:45	lunch
	1:15	break
	2:00	work-practice
	4:00	clean up
	4:15	sitting
	5:15	chanting
	5:30	supper
Evenings	6:00	break
	7:30	sitting (once weekly a talk is given by the teacher or a senior student)
	9:00	Sitting ends.

Indeed we are running away all the time to avoid coming face to face with our real selves.
—Anonymous, *Way of a Pilgrim*

Notice that most of the sitting is done mornings and evenings, which are relatively quieter times of the day, when work has either not yet begun or has been completed. A schedule like this obviates complex decisions as to how individuals should use their time, and lets each trainee develop a smooth rhythm for his or her day's training.

Then too, work-practice (J:*samu*),—be it gardening, buying groceries, or editing a book—is more than simply work in the usual sense of getting the chores done. Rather, like every aspect of the life of Zen practice, *samu* is itself a form of sitting.

Washing dishes, for instance, can be sheer drudgery; we can stand at the sink impatiently trying to get it over with, resenting every minute we have to devote to such menial labor. Isn't that the way we often tackle our chores?

But there is also another way of washing dishes, in which each act is done with the same intensity of concentration and awareness we devote to zazen. Scraping off the scraps, immersing the dishes in water, rinsing them of all traces of dirt and soap, drying them and stacking them neatly in the cabinet ready for use at the next meal— this can be powerful sitting. And as we become more completely involved in the task, the irritating consciousness of a gap between "I" and "what" "I" "want" "to do" is eliminated— dissolved like so much grease in the hot soapy water of non-dualistic practice. This is "just dishwashing," not "mere, lowly dishwashing,"

but dishwashing *only*. Just as when we "just sit" there is no problem or disharmony, so when we "just wash dishes" we find it to be excellent, harmonious practice.

And this work-practice is not limited to a Zen center or monastery. Going to school, building a house, turning a wrench, filling out a form at the office—all can be done with the same singleminded attentiveness. And even amidst the busiest of lives, time can be found to sit with others. Practicing like this in the everyday world, we come to be in harmony with that world itself, and to realize clearly that the community includes all beings everywhere.

44

When hungry, I eat; when tired, I sleep.
Fools laugh at me. The wise understand.
—Lin-chi I-hsüan (Rinzai Gigen),
Zen master (d. 866 A.D.)

How wondrous, how mysterious!
I carry fuel, I draw water.
      —P'ang Chu-shih,
      (eighth century A.D.)

Emmett Ho

Training Period

Unlike the Christian monastery in the West, a Zen monastery is not intended to be a lifelong place of seclusion in which people live a drastically different life than they would on the "outside." In some ways, the traditional Zen monastery has more the function of a cross between a seminary and a training camp, at which men and women prepare for the priesthood and train themselves for their lifelong practice in the "secular" world.

Typically, a monk or nun in Japan will spend two 90-day training periods each year in the monastery, and in the course of three to five years will become the head of a temple and leave the monastery more or less permanently. It is also not uncommon for laypersons to enter monasteries for short periods of time, ranging from a few days to a few months, to partake of a training refresher course. So during the year, a Japanese monastery actually operates on a full training schedule only about half the time.

Most of the training centers that have emerged in the West follow more or less the Japanese monastic pattern. During the training period, the daily schedule of activities is expanded to place a somewhat stronger emphasis on sitting (as much as four or five hours daily in some cases); additional talks are given by the teacher; and more individual study and interview time is scheduled for the trainees. Of course, in the Far East, this kind of training is predominantly intended for monks and nuns. But in the West, most training-program participants are actually laypersons. Temporarily setting aside the usual routines of their lives, they seem to find new awareness of their own strength and flexibility, and the perspective which emerges through training often helps them deal more creatively with families, friends and fellow-workers.

In such cases, monks, nuns and lay students may practice side by side, finding in their differences and similarities a constant challenge to make their time together one of mutual learning and growth.

Each month of the training period usually culminates in a *sesshin* or intensive sitting retreat, which is the third basic form of formal Zen training.

Sesshin

For three to seven days, the trainees live, eat, sit, work and sleep inside the monastery or Zen center. The emphasis is on sitting, about eight to ten hours daily at most places, but there is also work-practice, chanting, talks by the teacher, and daily personal encounters between master and student. The rule of silence is generally observed, and any socializing, even normal eye contact, is discouraged. Participants are usually urged to avoid any reading or writing during that time, and of course radio, TV and records are completely set aside. The time is to be used in the constant probing and exploration of one's own depths, and the rule of practice is to do whatever the schedule calls for in unison and silent harmony.

Paul Turner

Painted cakes do not satisfy hunger.
—Hsiang-yen Chih-hsien,
Zen master (814-890 A.D.)

The day begins early, around 4:00 a.m., and ends around 9:30 p.m. Almost every moment of the day is set aside for some specific activity, with the understanding that those attending the sesshin will participate as fully in each of the scheduled activities as they possibly can.

A typical day's schedule during sesshin might go something like this:

Morning	4:00	wake up
	4:30	Sitting (while sitting is going on, students have individual interviews with the Zen master)
	6:30	chanting
	7:00	breakfast
	8:00	work-practice
	9:35	clean up
	10:00	sitting (with interviews)
	11:15	chanting
	12:00	lunch
Afternoon	12:30	rest or free sitting
	2:00	sitting
	2:30	formal talk by teacher
	3:20	sitting
	4:30	chanting
	4:40	supper
	5:30	rest or free sitting
Evening	6:30	sitting (with interviews)
	9:00	sitting ends
	9:30	lights out

The word *sesshin* itself is revealing, for it literally means "to collect" or "to regulate the mind." This refers to the individual's experience of going deeper and deeper into his own noisy silence, and the bringing of order out of chaos as the sesshin concentration deepens and the sense of integration gets stronger.

But another meaning or implication of the word sesshin is "to join or link minds." This aspect of sesshin is a reflection of the group practice, for even as the group is made up of individuals with seemingly minimal contact with each other, still as the week goes on, there is created a pervasive sense of group identity and solidarity, within which personal idiosyncracies and peculiarities are at once subordinated and expressed. It is common for us in the West to see individual and group identities as polar opposites, and we tend to feel that we must choose between them. But in sesshin, it becomes clear that both are real and compatible, and that the deepest harmony occurs when both are accorded the right appreciation and expression.

Intrinsically, sesshin is a model of life itself, and requires that the community meet its own needs and recognize its own nature. There are certain arrangements which need to be made for feeding and housing the participants, there are the procedures by which the zendo is run smoothly, and there is the underlying unity of all those who practice together. There may be many individual differences of personality, style, taste and maturity; yet in sesshin, the diversity becomes harmony as the participants move through the hours of the day together, sitting, working, eating, studying and sleeping according to the schedule, with a minimum of friction.

Experientially, it's a lot like boiling water on the stove. By turning up the flame and not moving the kettle away from the heat, the water soon reaches boiling point. In following the schedule with all one's might, one is turning up the heat and leaving the kettle on the fire. At some precise moment, the water will boil. That is the moment of the breakthrough, when we appreciate our true nature directly. It's very interesting to see it happening; the sesshin process is the opposite of a vicious circle. As we practice together, going through all kinds of adjustments and difficulties, we slowly begin to experience our unity. As we experience it, two things happen. On the one hand, we tend to create that very state of mind itself, in which we are able to see the oneness; simultaneously, we are strengthening and expressing it as we give rise to it. And as we see each other strengthening and expressing it more and more, so it tends to be created anew. Perhaps we could call this a benign circle.

So sesshin leads the Zen student through the thick undergrowth of confusion and scattered energies, across the quicksand of ego-tripping and over the chasm of dualistic thought. It is a rugged and sobering trek, with deep valleys and high peaks. But it is in the making of the journey that the individual and the community discover and create themselves continuously from mo-

In studying ourselves, we find the harmony that is our total existence. We do not make harmony. We do not achieve or gain it. It is there all the time. Here we are, in the midst of this perfect way, and our practice is simply to realize it and then to actualize it in our everyday life.
—Taizan Maezumi Roshi

ment to moment.

Through it all the teacher serves as a guide, for he has himself covered this ground thoroughly many times before, and he especially knows the snares and pitfalls awaiting the novice. It is the teacher's responsibility to assess the needs of the individual and the group, and accordingly to regulate the pace and the rigor of the sesshin to provide the optimum level of challenge and stimulation. Through his senior assistants, the teacher keeps the sesshin focussed and running smoothly, and through the frequent daily encounters he has with each individual, the teacher gets feedback about how everyone is doing, individually and collectively.

Of course, it is also true that in a sense everyone is the teacher of everyone else. When you sit with a group you soon begin to sense a remarkable supportive energy which comes into being, and which affects all those in its field. So as your sitting-neighbor helps you, you in turn also help him.

Then too, sesshin relieves individuals of the need to break concentration even briefly. Most of the time we all have very busy lives, with dozens of decisions and thoughts demanding our attention moment after moment. But since every activity during sesshin is scheduled, all we need do is follow the schedule as closely as we can, and the whole issue of self-discipline, busyness, and distraction is resolved. When the schedule calls for lunch, then we go to lunch; when it says zazen, then we go and sit. And because most of the activities of the day are done in a rather formal manner (that is, in a prescribed, standard way), even such minor decisions as how to take your seat or which bowl to eat from are all obviated in advance by the very form itself.

Naturally, most of us would not wish to live by a formal sesshin schedule all the time. But attending sesshin regularly during the year can bring a person very close to himself, and can build great strength and self-confidence. Moreover, we can really get a sense of how precious our time is.

Experiencing Sesshin

Most people report that their first sesshin is a most unsettling experience.

First of all, no one speaks or even makes eye-contact with anyone else. In fact, most of the normal social amenities have been set aside: no one greets you with a cheerful "hello;" no one acknowledges your presence as you pass others in the zendo or around the grounds; everyone seems to be preoccupied with some weighty matter. All of this may prove anxiety-provoking, especially if you rely heavily on polite social chit-chat to establish your status and identity, and to make you feel more comfortable.

And although the strangeness will gradually wear off, that initial insecurity and degree of disorientation may give you a clue as to how far from stability and harmony the so-called "normal" way of life actually is.

For the first three days of sesshin, the physical adjustment is also quite rigorous. The muscles of the body, used to very different patterns of activity and repose, must now accommodate themselves to lengthy periods of immobility and the stress of maintaining zazen many hours more each day than they are normally used to.

But sometime between the third and fourth days, there is a point at which discomfort and fatigue peak. If, at such a juncture, you just avoid drawing any conclusions (such as "I can't stand this any more" or "I'm never going to make it" or "This isn't so tough; maybe I don't have to try so hard."), and continue to practice with steady concentration, a corner will be turned. There is a curious and most welcome "second wind" which comes about the third or fourth day, and from that point onward, time seems to accelerate enormously to the end of ses-shin. By the third or fourth day, too, the body has greatly adjusted to the physical stresses, and the discomfort or pain have become more famil-iar and less overwhelming, so that there is a real feeling of having gotten over the hump.

At this point, sesshin may become very closely integrated into oneself, so that there is no sep-aration between the demands of the sesshin schedule and one's own personal needs and rhythms.

Harmony cannot exist without the state of maintaining balance . . . When forty or fifty people get together to try individually to balance body and mind, then group harmony can be established.
—Taizan Maezumi Roshi

55

Realizing the Harmony

Perhaps this process of reaching a crisis and then passing through it into calm waters is characteristic not only of sitting sesshin, but of all the other aspects of life as well.

For there generally comes a day when you walk into that silent room with all the zafus neatly lined up and the faint smell of incense in the air, and you feel welcome and at home.

As the others come in and take their seats, there is no longer a nagging sense of "what shall I say now?", for the real communication is saying itself with each inhalation and exhalation.

What has happened?

One thing may be that you are beginning to experience the harmony of community, knowing that it doesn't depend on conversation or on bridging gaps. There is no need either to gloss over differences or to create polite distractions. The harmony is realized as we sit together.

In a way, it's even misleading to speak of sitting alone or together. No matter how many people are sitting in the room, there is still only that great reality with each sitter at its exact center. In that sense, since each one is the whole universe, each one is always alone. The "whole universe" is always alone, since it includes everything and everyone throughout space and time. There is nothing outside of it to keep it (you) company.

But at the same time, and by the same token, nobody ever sits alone, since each of us contains the infinite diversity and variety of all reality.

It is the realization that these two seemingly opposite perspectives are mutually compatible —are, in fact the same thing—that allows us to enter into the spirit of community together.

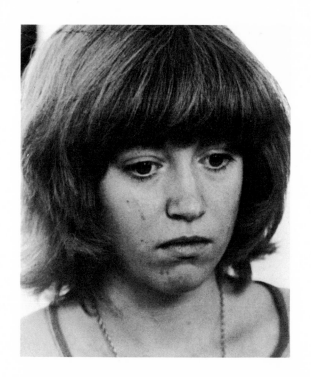

*To connect our mind and the Mind of
the universe is what sesshin means.*
—Taizan Maezumi Roshi

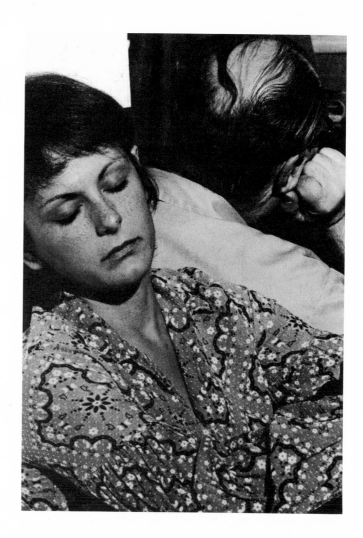

AFTERWORD

At the end of a book it is tempting to tie it all up neatly with a conclusion. This book, however, has no conclusion, being a book of beginnings.

You are already writing the remainder of the book, which, although invisible, is endless.

A final word of encouragement: whatever happens in your life/practice, just take note of it and keep on going.

Remember who you are, and keep on going.

And forget about that, and keep on going.

Do I contradict myself?
Very well then I contradict myself,
I am large, I contain multitudes.
—Walt Whitman

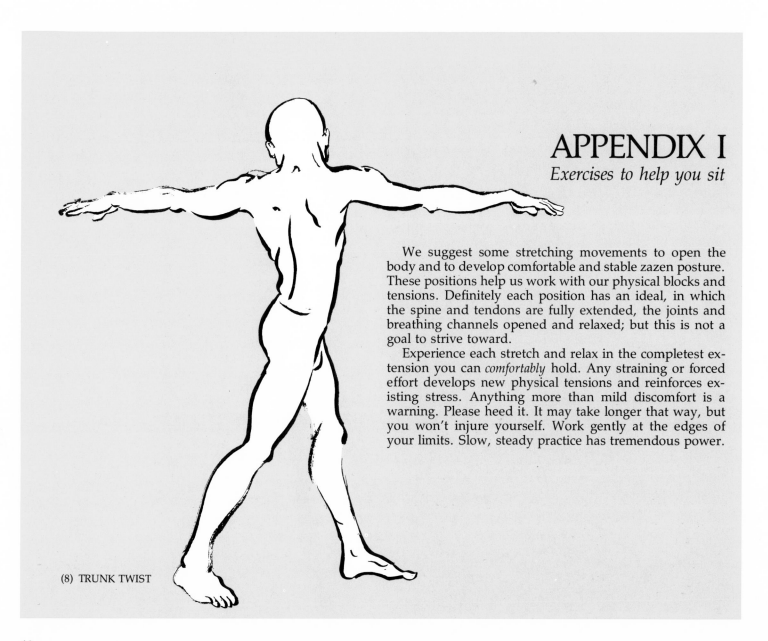

APPENDIX I
Exercises to help you sit

We suggest some stretching movements to open the body and to develop comfortable and stable zazen posture. These positions help us work with our physical blocks and tensions. Definitely each position has an ideal, in which the spine and tendons are fully extended, the joints and breathing channels opened and relaxed; but this is not a goal to strive toward.

Experience each stretch and relax in the completest extension you can *comfortably* hold. Any straining or forced effort develops new physical tensions and reinforces existing stress. Anything more than mild discomfort is a warning. Please heed it. It may take longer that way, but you won't injure yourself. Work gently at the edges of your limits. Slow, steady practice has tremendous power.

(8) TRUNK TWIST

1) BUTTERFLY—Sit up straight on the ground. Put the soles of the feet together, hold the toes with your hands and bring the heels into the groin as close as comfortably possible. Work the knees up and down. This loosens the

legs and hips. Then, keeping the back straight, lean over the feet. In holding this and other postures, do not tense the muscles. Inhale deeply and exhale in a long "ahhhh." This helps release the tendons and joints.

(1) BUTTERFLY

2) HEAD-KNEE—Sit up straight on the ground, legs stretched out and together. Keeping the arms straight and the back of the legs flat on the ground, reach for the toes. Lean down slowly with the lower back still straight. When you are as far down as is comfortable, hold the legs or the toes for support. Again, relax the muscles and breathe from the lower abdomen while holding this position.

(2) HEAD-KNEE

3) LEG SPREAD—Sit up straight on the ground, legs stretched out in front. Stretch the legs apart as wide as is comfortable. Keeping the back straight and bracing yourself with your hands, lean forward and down as far as is comfortable. Breathe into the lower abdomen. Come back up. Keeping the spine straight, lean the left side over the left leg, hold and concentrate on breathing. Come back up. Keeping the spine straight, lean over towards the right leg; hold and concentrate on breathing.

(3) LEG SPREAD

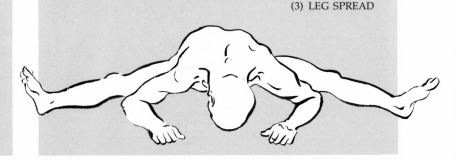

4) NECK HANGS—(Not Shown) Sit in a comfortable position with the back straight and relaxed. Hang the head forward and concentrate on breathing into the back of the neck and between the shoulder blades. Hang the head to the left with the ear directly over the left shoulder, while concentrating on breathing into the right side of the neck and the right shoulder. Hang the head to the right with the ear directly over the right shoulder, while concentrating on breathing into the left side of the neck and the left shoulder. Let the head hang back while concentrating on breathing into the thorax.

5) NECK TWIST—(Not Shown) Sitting comfortably, keep the head upright and turn the head to the left and right several times. Then turn the head to the left and hold, feeling the breathing in the front of the chest. Turn to the right and hold, feeling the breathing in the front of the chest.

6) NECK ROTATIONS—(Not Shown) Slowly rotate the head several times counterclockwise 360°. Then rotate clockwise several times.

7) ARM SWING—(Not Shown) Standing comfortably with the feet parallel, let the hands hang in front of the hips, palms facing each other. Keep the arms slightly in front of the body and swing the arms out to the side. Swing the right arm out to the right and the left arm out to the left. The upswing should reach just above the head, and in the downswing the wrists should cross in front of the pelvis.

8) TRUNK TWIST—(See page 63) Stand with the left foot forward and the right foot about three feet back and turned to the side at a 70° angle. Facing in the direction of your left foot, stretch the arms out to the sides horizontally, palms down. Gently turn from side to side feeling the turn through the shoulders, the back, the hips and legs. Then reverse this, putting the right foot forward and the left foot about three feet back and turned to the side. Facing in the direction of your right foot, stretch the arms out horizontally, to the sides palms down. Gently turn from side to side, feeling the turn through the whole body.

9) LEG STRETCH—Sit in the Burmese, half-lotus or full lotus position. Gently lower your torso in the direction of one knee until it begins to get uncomfortable. Don't strain to reach it. Hold for a count of ten, straighten up, relax, and repeat. Repeat the exercise for one minute with each knee.

(9) LEG STRETCH

10) LEG STRETCH—Sit with the left leg stretched out in front of you. Fold the right leg so the top of the foot is on the thigh of the outstretched leg. Gently press the knee toward the ground for a count of ten. Then switch legs.

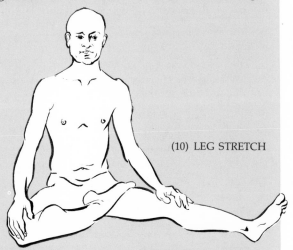

(10) LEG STRETCH

11) LIFTING THE WEIGHT—(Not Shown) Lie flat on your back on the floor. Make sure your abdomen isn't constricted by a belt or tight clothing. Then take a brick, or a small bag of sugar or sand—any three to five pound weight will do—and place it on your abdomen below the navel. Now watch the weight rise as you inhale, and fall as you exhale. Notice how far the weight moves up and down.

Now, using *only* the belly muscles, see if you can make the weight rise higher on the inhalation, and sink deeper on the exhalation. Take your time and don't rush. Feel which muscles are involved. Do this for two or three minutes.

Then immediately get into your sitting position, and as you breathe, notice that the same abdominal muscles are used as in the exercise. After doing this for a few days just before you sit, you should develop a far clearer "feel" for the lower abdominal wall.

Suggested fabric for covering: A sturdy material such as a cotton/polyester blend.

Suggested stuffing: Kapok.

BASIC PIECES:

a) Length of cloth 59 inches long, 6 inches to 9 inches wide (depending on how high you would like your cushion to be).

b) Two circles of cloth, each with a diameter of 11 inches to 13 inches (depending on how large around you would like your cushion to be).

STEP 1. Pleat the length of cloth. There should be fourteen ¾ inch pleats, 3 inches apart. To pleat:

a) Beginning 6½ inches from the left edge of the length, make three marks, ¾ inch apart, thus marking out the first pleat:

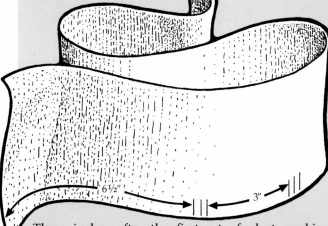

Three inches after the first set of pleat markings, make the second set, as indicated above. Continue doing this till you have 14 pleats. When you finish, the last pleat marking should be 3 inches from the right edge. (If you wish to have narrower pleats, of course, simply increase the number of pleats.)

b) Next, iron the pleats and pin them. They should all be folded and ironed in toward the left-hand side. For each set of pleat markings, fold the third in toward the first, as shown:

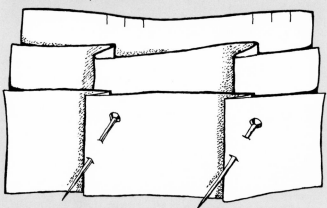

Pin as shown above.

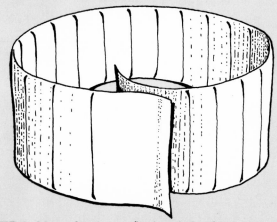

STEP 2. Now, having completed the first step, take the right edge of the pleated strip of cloth and pin it to the left end of the strip, 3¼ inches from the left edge.

STEP 3. Mark each circle of cloth at four equidistant points.

Turn pleated length of cloth inside out.

Pin each circle to the pleated strip, one circle to the top edge and one to the bottom edge, at each of the four points.

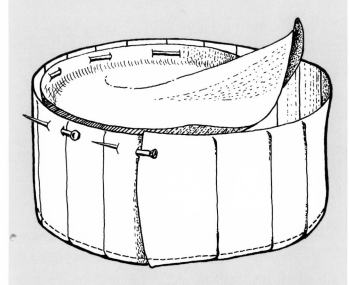

STEP 4. Next, ease (pin) all the pleats in to the circles, top and bottom. Sew the circles to the length of cloth.

APPENDIX II
How to Make Your Own Zafu

STEP 5. Turn inside out and stuff with kapok (through opening in the side that the zafu will have).

VOILA!

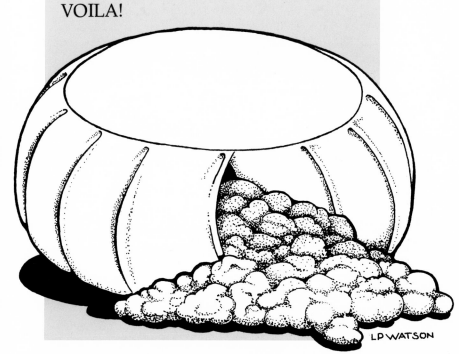

LP WATSON

ARIZONA

Tibetan Vajrayana
    Buddhist Group
4004 E. McKellips
Mesa, AZ 85203
(Nyingma Institute
    Affiliate)

Tibetan Vajrayana
    Buddhist Group
4750 N. Camino Corto
Tucson, AZ 85719
(Nyingma Institute
    Affiliate)

CALIFORNIA

Berkeley Buddhist Priory
3538 Telegraph Ave.
Oakland, CA 94609
(415) 655-1286
(Shasta Abbey Affiliate)

Berkeley Zendo (a,b)
1670 Dwight Way
Berkeley, CA 94703
(415) 845-2403

Cimarron Zen Center of
    Rinzai-Ji (b,c)
2505 Cimarron
Los Angeles, CA
(213) 732-2263

City of 10,000 Buddhas
P.O. Box 217
Talmage, CA 95481
(Gold Mountain Monastery
    Affiliate)

Dharmadhatu
2288 Fulton
Berkeley, CA 94704
(Vajradhatu Affiliate)

Dharmadhatu
26120 W. Fremont Rd.
Los Altos Hills, CA 94022
(415) 948-7211
(Vajradhatu Affiliate)

Dharmadhatu
57 Hartford St.
San Francisco, CA 94114
(415) 863-6578
(Vajradhatu Affiliate)

Dharmadhatu
828 Chapala St. #204
Santa Barbara, CA 93101
(805) 965-4039
(Vajradhatu Affiliate)

Dharmadhatu
1753 Cloverfield Blvd.
Santa Monica, CA 90404
(213) 828-2855
(Vajradhatu Affiliate)

Genjo-Ji (a,b)
6367 Sonoma Mt. Rd.
Santa Rosa, CA 95404

Gold Mountain Monastery
1731 15th Street   (a,b)
San Francisco, CA

Gold Wheel Temple
5743 Huntington Dr. N.
Los Angeles, CA 90032
(Gold Mountain Monastery
    Affiliate)

Haiku Zendo (a,b)
c/o Bodhi
Box 638
Los Altos, CA 94022
(Bodhi Affiliate)

International Buddhist
    Meditation Center (a)
928 So. New Hampshire
    Ave.
Los Angeles, CA 90006
(213) 384-0850

Joshu Zen Temple (b)
2305 Harriman Ln.
Redondo Beach, CA
(Zen Center of Rinzai-ji
    Affiliate)

Long Beach Zen Center
1942 Magnolia
Long Beach, CA
(Zen Buddhist Temple,
    Chicago, Affiliate)

Mt. Baldy Zen Center (b,c)
P.O. Box 429
Mt. Baldy, CA 91759
(Zen Center of Rinzai-ji
    Affiliate)

Nyingma Institute (a,b)
1815 Highland Place
Berkeley, CA 94709

Saginaw Zen Priory
32646 Saginaw West Road
Cottage Grove, CA 97424
(503) 942-7515
(Shasta Abbey Affiliate)

Santa Cruz Zendo (b,c)
113 School St.
Santa Cruz, CA 95060
(Bodhi Affiliate)

Shasta Abbey (a,b)
P.O. Box 478
Mt. Shasta, CA 96067
(916) 926-4208

Society of the Smiling
    Buddha (b)
P.O. Box 590
La Jolla, CA 92038

Spring Mountain Sangha
    (b,c)
11525 Mid-Mountain Rd.
Potter Valley, CA 95469
(Bodhi Affiliate)

Tahl Mah Sah Zen Center
354 So. Kingsley Dr.
Los Angeles, CA 90020
(213) 380-5312
(Providence Zen Center
    Affiliate)

Tibetan Nyingma
    Meditation Center
2425 Hillside Ave.
Berkeley, CA 94704
(Nyingma Institute
    Affiliate)

Zen Center (a,b)
300 Page Street
San Francisco, CA 94102

Zen Center of Los Angeles
927 South Normandie Ave.
Los Angeles, CA 90006 (a,b)

COLORADO

Karma Dzong (b,c)
1345 Spruce Street
Boulder, CO 80302
(303) 444-0190
(Vajradhatu Affiliate)

Rocky Mountain Dharma
    Center (b,c)
Route 1
Livermore, CO 80536
(303) 881-2372
(Vajradhatu Affiliate)

Tibetan Vajrayana
    Buddhist Group
1441 Broadway
Boulder, CO 80302
(Nyingma Institute Affiliate)

CONNECTICUT

New Haven Zen Center
193 Mansfield Street
New Haven, CT 06511
(Providence Zen Center
    Affiliate)

HAWAII

Diamond Sangha (a,b)
Maui Zendo
RR #1 Box 702
Haiku, Hawaii 96708

Koko An Zendo (b,c)
2119 Kaloa Way
Honolulu, Hawaii 96822
(Diamond Sangha Affiliate)

ILLINOIS

Dharmadhatu
640 N. State Street
Chicago, IL 60610
(312) 649-9892
(Vajradhatu Affiliate)

Zen Buddhist Temple (a,b)
2230 North Halsted Street
Chicago, IL 60614
(312) DI8-1218

INDIANA

Lafayette Indiana Zazen
    Group (b)
236 Harrison St.
W. Lafayette, Indiana
Contact: Liz Kuster
(317) 743-2788
(MZMC Affiliate)

IOWA

Iowa City Zen Group (b)
Wesley House
120 No. Dubuque
Iowa City, Iowa
Contact: Glen L. Kellogg
    (319) 337-7677
(MZMC Affiliate)

MASSACHUSETTS

Cambridge Zen Center (b,c)
7 Ashfort Terrace
Allston, MA 02134
(Providence Zen Center
Affiliate)

Chestnut Hill Zendo (b,c)
4 Travis Dr.
Chestnut Hill, MA
(Cambridge Buddhist
    Association Affiliate)

Dharmadhatu
169 B Upland Rd.
Cambridge, MA 02140
(617) 492-8099
    and 661-7118
(Vajradhatu Affiliate)

Sim Gum Do Zen Sword
    Center
1112 Boylston St.
Boston, MA 02115
(Providence Zen Center
Affiliate)

MICHIGAN

Matava Zen Center (a,b)
2093 California St.
Saginaw, MI 48601
(517) 777-5890

MINNESOTA

Minnesota Zen Meditation
    Center (MZMC) (a,b)
3413 Girard Ave. So.
Minneapolis, Minn 55408

NEBRASKA

Omaha Zen Group (b)
1915 N. 84th St.
Omaha, Neb 68114
Contact: John Marquez
(402) 393-4842 or 397-0814
(MZMC Affiliate)

NEW MEXICO

Jemez Bodhi Mandala (a,b)
Box 44
Jemez Springs, NM 87025
(Rinzai-ji Affiliate)

NEW YORK

Buffalo Zen Group (a,b)
629 Deerfield Dr.
N. Tonawanda, NY 14120

APPENDIX III

*Some Meditation Centers in the United States,
Canada and England*

It is easier to practice with the support of others, so
we've provided a listing of sitting groups in the United
States, Canada and England. Those listed here are the
ones whose addresses we were able to find and who
responded to a letter from us asking if they wished to be
listed and if they had a regular schedule and a full- or
part-time teacher*.

The symbols which follow the name of an
organization are:

(*a.*) Full-time teacher in residence
(*b.*) Regular meditation schedule
(*c.*) Part-time teacher

*It is impossible to ascertain what the term *teacher* means
to different people. Therefore, no particular level of
qualification is implied by the use of this term.

Dharmadhatu
78 Fifth Ave.
New York, NY 10011
(212) 675-1561
(Vajradhatu Affiliate)

International Zen Center
105 E. 16th St.
New York, NY 10003
(Providence Zen Center
   Affiliate)

The Zen Center (a,b)
7 Arnold Park
Rochester, NY 14607

Dai Bosatsu Zendo (a,b)
The Zen Studies Society,
   Inc.
Beecher Lake, Star Route
Livingston Manor, NY
   12758

New York Zendo
The Zen Studies Society,
   Inc.
223 East 67th St.
New York, NY 10021

NORTH CAROLINA

North Carolina Zen Center
   (a,b)
Rt. 1 Box 52
Pittsboro, NC 27312

RHODE ISLAND

The Providence Zen
   Center (a,b)
K.B.C. Hong Poep Won
48 Hope St.
Providence, RI 02903

TEXAS

Dharmadhatu
806 Baylor St.
Austin, TX 78703
(512) 477-6669
(Vajradhatu Affiliate)

VERMONT

Karmê-Choling
Star Route
Barnet, VT 05821
(802) 633-2384 and 633-
   4417
(Vajradhatu Affiliate)

WASHINGTON, DC

Dharmadhatu
3220 Idaho Ave. N.W.
Washington, DC 20016
(202) 686-5307
(Vajradhatu Affiliate)

The Zen Buddhist Group
   of Washington, DC (b,c)
The Zen Studies Society,
   Inc.
1717 P St. N.W.
Washington, DC 20036

WASHINGTON STATE

University of Washington
   Zazen Kai (a,b)
c/o Dr. G. Webb DM-10
Univ. of Washington
Seattle, WA 98105

CANADA AND
ENGLAND

The Mouse Hole Buddist
   Group (a,b)
Penaluna Clodgy Moor
Paul, Penzance TR 19 6UR
Cornwall, England
(Shasta Abbey Affiliate)

The Buddhist Society (a,b)
58 Eccleston Square
London SWI, England

Dharma House (a,b)
8 Radford Rd.
Lewishah, London, S.E. B.
   England
01-318 4699
(Shasta Abbey Affiliate)

Throssel Hole Priory
Carr Shield NR. Hexhan
Northumberland NE 47 AL
England
(Shasta Abbey Affiliate)

Dharmadhatu
1429 Pierce Street
Montreal 254
Quebec, Canada
(514) 935-3948
(Vajradhatu Affiliate)

Dharmadhatu
269 Richmond St. W.
Toronto, Ontario
Canada M5V IXI
(416) 884-3619
(Vajradhatu Affiliate)

PAGE

3 Source unknown.

5 Translated by the editors.

7 Minor White, *Mirrors, Messages, Manifestations,* (Millerton, New York: Aperture, Inc., 1969), p. 41.

9 Hakuyu Taizan Maezumi and Bernard Tetsugen Glassman, ed., *On Zen Practice II: Body Breath and Mind,* (Los Angeles: Zen Center of Los Angeles, Inc., 1976), p. 55.

13 Walt Whitman, *Leaves of Grass,* (New York: The New American Library, 1962), p. 64.

15 Taizan Maezumi Roshi, "Sooner or Later You Come to a Real Dead End (An Interview)," *Laughing Man,* vol.1, no.1, p. 23.

17 Traditional.

19 Shunryu Suzuki, *Zen Mind, Beginner's Mind,* (New York: John Weatherhill, Inc., 1970), p. 27. (Reprinted by permission of Zen Center)

21 Maezumi, *On Zen Practice II,* p. 63.

25 Soyen Shaku, "The First Step in Zazen," trans. Nyogen Senzaki, in *Daily Sutras,* (New York: The New York Zendo of the Zen Studies Society), p. 82.

27 Suzuki, *Zen Mind, Beginner's Mind,* p. 29.

29 Suzuki, *Zen Mind, Beginner's Mind,* p. 35.

31 Lewis Carroll, "The Walrus and the Carpenter," in *A Nonsense Anthology,* ed. Carolyn Wells, (New York: Dover Publications, Inc., 1958), p. 95.

33 Stanley Hendricks, ed., *Emerson: Selections,* (Kansas City, Missouri: Hallmark, 1969), p. 54.

35 Aldous Huxley, *The Doors of Perception* and *Heaven and Hell,* (New York: Harper & Row, Colophon Books, 1954), p. 7.

39 T.S. Eliot, "The Dry Salvages," *The Complete Poems and Plays: 1909–1950,* (New York: Harcourt Brace Jovanovich, 1958), p. 136.

NOTES

45 Irmgard Schloegl, *The Wisdom of the Zen Masters,* (London: Sheldon Press, 1975), p. 55.

48 Traditional.

51 Translated by the editors.

53 Hakuyu Taizan Maezumi and Bernard Tetsugen Glassman, ed., *On Zen Practice,* (Los Angeles: Zen Center of Los Angeles, Inc., 1976), p. 41.

55 Maezumi, *On Zen Practice,* p. 36.

57 Ibid., p. 33.

62 Whitman, *Leaves of Grass,* p. 96.

To be enlightened by all things
is to free one's body and mind
and those of others.

No trace of enlightenment remains,
and this no-trace continues endlessly.

Dōgen Zenji (1200-1253)
Shōbōgenzō: Genjokoan

John Daishin Buksbazen, *Publishing Editor of the Zen Writings series, and head of Zen Center of Los Angeles publications, serves as vice president and pastoral counselor as well as instructor for the Introductory Seminars in Zen practice at ZCLA. He was installed as shuso (head training monk) at the 1974 summer training period. Formerly an actor, writer and social worker, he received a B.S. degree from the Temple University School of Communication & Theater, and has done graduate work in counseling and psychotherapy at California State University and the Southern California Counseling Center.*

John Daido Loori *is first and foremost a teacher of seeing. Art Director of the Zen Writings series, he has been presenting lectures and workshops on Zen photography for the past six years. His work has been extensively exhibited on the East Coast, and has appeared in such publications as* Aperture *and* Time-Life Photography. *He studied photography with Minor White, and Zen with Muishitsu Eido Roshi in New York, and is presently working on a book,* The Art of Mindful Photography, *at the Zen Center of Los Angeles, where he is continuing his studies with Taizan Maezumi Roshi.*

Peter Ishin Matthiessen *is a student of Zen as well as a naturalist and a novelist. He is the author of* At Play in the Fields of the Lord, The Tree Where Man Was Born, *and the best-selling novel* Far Tortuga.

Chōtan Aitken Roshi, *a Dharma successor of Kōun Yamada Roshi in the Harada/Yasutani line of succession, heads the Diamond Sangha in Hawaii, which includes the Koko-an Zen group in Honolulu and the Maui Zendo.*

The Paulownia leaves-and-flowers design is traditional in Japan, where in slightly different form, it serves as the crest of Sōjiji Monastery, one of two headquarters temples of the Soto School of Zen Buddhism. In the form shown here, it is the crest of Kōshinji Temple in Ōtawara, whose Abbot, the Venerable Hakujun Kuroda Roshi, was Maezumi Roshi's principal Soto teacher. In the United States, it represents Zen Center of Los Angeles, publishers of the Zen Writings series.

Library of Congress Cataloguing in Publication Data
Buksbazen, John Daishin, 1939-
    To forget the self.
(The Zen writings series; 3)
1. Meditation (Zen Buddhism) I. Title. II. Series.
BQ9288.B84   294.5'43   76-9463
ISBN 0-916820-03-3